Drums for the Absolute Beginner

Absolutely everything you need to know to start playing now!

Pete Sweeney

Alfred, the leader in educational publishing, and the National Guitar Workshop, one of America's finest guitar schools, have joined forces to bring you the best, most progressive educational tools possible. We hope you will enjoy this book and encourage you to look for other fine products from Alfred and the National Guitar Workshop.

Alfred Publishing Co., Inc.
16320 Roscoe Blvd., Suite 100
P.O. Box 10003
Van Nuys, CA 91410-0003
alfred.com

This book was acquired, edited and produced by Workshop Arts, Inc., the publishing arm of the National Guitar Workshop.
Nathaniel Gunod, acquisitions and editor
Michael Rodman, editor
Gary Tomassetti, music typesetter
Timothy Phelps, interior design
CD recorded at Bar None Studios, Northford, CT
Cover drumset photograph courtesy of Yamaha Corporation of America

ISBN-10: 0-7390-2366-7 (Book)
ISBN-13: 978-0-7390-2366-2 (Book)

ISBN-10: 0-7390-2367-5 (Book & CD)
ISBN-13: 978-0-7390-2367-9 (Book & CD)

Table of Contents

Track 1

A compact disc is included with this book. This disc can make learning with the book easier and more enjoyable. This symbol will appear next to every exercise that is on the CD. Use the CD to help ensure that you are capturing the feel of the exercises, interpreting the rhythms correctly, and so on. The track numbers next the symbols correspond directly to the exercise you want to hear. Track 1 explains how the CD works. Have fun!

About the Author

Pete Sweeney has been a professional musician since 1983. He has studied with Dave Calarco, Joe Morello and other notable drummers. He has also attended the Drummer's Collective in New York City.

Pete has been a faculty member at the National Guitar Workshop since 1993. He has performed with many great musicians, such as Duke Robillard, Ronnie Earl, Mick Goodrick, Frank Gambale, Nick Brignola and Johnny "Clyde" Copeland.

Pete has also toured the United States and Canada with various musical groups and has appeared on CDs featuring a wide variety of musical styles, including big band, rock, funk and jazz. He recently toured with former Allman Brothers guitarist "Dangerous" Dan Toler and Ireland's Tony Kenny. Pete has performed on a Grammy-nominated CD with Jay Traynor and the Joey Thomas big band, and he can be heard on the soundtrack for the Miramax motion picture "The Castle."

Pete endorses Vic Firth sticks, Sabian cymbals and Aquarian drumheads. He lives in Chatham, New York.

Acknowledgments

I would like to thank Neil Larrivee at Vic Firth; Bob Boos, Terry Shaw and Joe Healy at Sabian; and Roy Burns and Chris Brady at Aquarian. I would also like to thank Nat Gunod, Matt Smith and Dave Smolover at the National Guitar Workshop; my parents, Patrick and Patricia Sweeney; my brother, Paul; my niece, Lacee and my wife, Robin. Special thanks to my teachers Dave Calarco and Joe Morello for their continual inspiration.

Other books and videos by Pete Sweeney:
- *Rock Drums for Beginners*, book with CD
- *30-Day Drum Workout*, book
- *Rock Drums for Beginners, Vol 1*, Video
- *Rock Drums for Beginners, Vol 2*, Video

Introduction

Welcome to *Drums for the Absolute Beginner*. If you've always wanted to play the drums, this is a great place to start. The lessons in this book take you from holding the sticks and reading rhythms to playing the rudiments, beats and fills that are the basis of every drummer's technique to learning the various instruments in the drumset.

Here are a few suggestions to keep in mind as you begin working through the book:

1. Once you find a *tempo* (playing speed) for an exercise, be careful not to speed up or slow down. If you want to play something faster or slower, stop and begin a new tempo. Being able to maintain a *steady* tempo is one of the most important skills a good drummer must have.

2. If you feel your hands getting stiff or tight, stop for a few minutes and relax.

3. Have fun! If you enjoy practicing, you'll do it longer and more often. Good luck!

Getting Started

● Parts of the Drumset

Here are some of the instruments and accessories that make up a drumset.

Tom-Tom—Drum mounted on the bass drum. Tom-toms vary in size from 8" to 16". The number of toms in a set may also vary from 1 to 3, or more. Sounds deeper than the snare.

Crash Cymbal—Cymbals used primarily for accents. They range in size from very small "splash" cymbals (6") to very large "crashes" (18").

Rim—Secures the drumhead in place.

Drumhead—Playing surface of the drum. Drumheads vary in thickness, weight and color.

Hi-Hat and Stand—The stand allows you to play the two hi-hat cymbals with your left foot. Simply lift your left foot for an open sound, press down for a closed sound. Rock drummers often hit the closed hi-hat with their sticks.

Ride Cymbal—Large cymbal, usually on the right side, used for continuous playing. The "bell" is located in the center. The ride cymbal sits on a stand.

Tension Rod—*Tensions* (tightens or loosens) the drumhead with the use of a drum key.

Lug—Holds the tension rod in place.

Seat (Throne) —This is the starting place—the whole set will be positioned around you.

Floor Tom—Drum suspended off the floor on legs. Sizes vary from 14" to 18". Lower-sounding than the tom-tom(s) but higher than the bass.

Snare Drum—Usually the highest-pitched drum of the set. A throw switch on the side of the drum (usually the left side) allows you to flip the wire snares on or off the bottom head. Note the difference in the sound with the snares on and off.

Bass Drum Pedal—Connected to the bottom rim of the bass drum, it allows you to play from a seated position. The pedal can be tensioned in various ways , usually by adjusting the spring.

Bass Drum—Sits on the floor with adjustable legs. The lowest-tuned drum of the set.

● Shopping for Your Drumset

If you've never purchased a drumset before, there are a few things you should know before setting out for the local music store. The drumset is really a group of individual instruments, and these instruments can be bought separately or as a package deal. First, determine what you can afford to spend. The price of a complete set of drums can range from moderately inexpensive to quite expensive. Here are a few suggestions to make shopping for a drumset a little easier.

Determine What Size Drumset is Right for You

Drumsets come in all shapes and sizes; some may have as many as ten tom-toms and two bass drums with eight cymbals. For the beginning drummer, a smaller, well-constructed set is a far better choice. The basic components of any drumset are the snare drum, bass drum and hi-hat. The traditional essential set usually includes the snare, bass and hi-hat, plus one mounted tom on the bass drum, a floor tom and two cymbals. The snare, cymbals, hi-hat and throne are supported by stands (which should be included with the set). The tom-tom is usually attached to the bass drum with a special piece of hardware, while the floor tom is suspended on a set of legs. The number of drums in your set is a personal choice, but this small setup is a good place to start.

Finding the Right-Sized Bass Drum

When looking for a drumset, it's important to find the bass drum that's the right size for your individual height and reach. Bass drums come in many sizes, from a small 18" to a large 24". If you're a small person and buy a 24" bass drum, you may have a difficult time reaching the mounted tom-toms. The larger the bass drum, the higher the toms have to be placed, and the less flexibility you'll have in setting them up. To determine what size will work best for you, go to a store that will allow you to sit behind a set and make adjustments.

New vs. Used

One alternative to buying new drums is to shop for a good used set. Do some research before you buy; look both in music stores, on the Internet and in classified ads. You should be able to find a good used set at a reasonable price. Make sure to thoroughly inspect all the drums, cymbals and hardware in any used set you're interested in buying. When buying a used set from a store, make sure you understand their return and exchange policies in case you run into problems with the set down the road.

● Parts of the Snare Drum

The snare drum takes its name from the wire snares that can be *tensioned* (tightened) against the resonant (bottom) head of the drum. These snares are tensioned by turning *snare adjustment screw* located on the side of the drum. The tension can be adjusted from loose to tight to produce a range of sounds. By using the *throw switch,* you can remove the snares from the bottom head, producing a tom-tom sound.

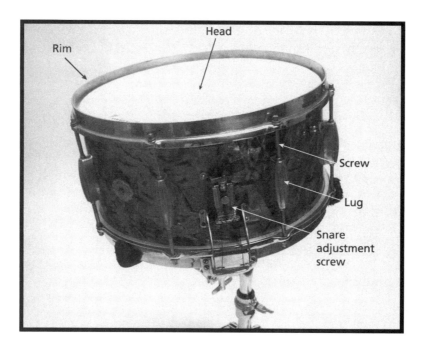

John Bonham *was the drummer for Led Zeppelin from the group's founding in 1968 until his death in 1980. His innovative recordings with Led Zeppelin continue to influence drummers today.*

● Tuning the Drums

One of the secrets to getting a good drum sound is making sure that all the *tension screws* that hold the rim and drumhead are equally tensioned all around the drum. Here are a few suggestions for achieving equal tension on your drums.

Start with a Good Drumhead

It's possible to make an old drumhead sound reasonably good, but it's far easier with a head that hasn't been worn out. If there are small holes or large dents in the head, it's a good idea to replace it. This will make a huge difference in how the drum will sound.

Tuning a New Drumhead

Once you've replaced the drumhead, put the rim on and replace the tuning screws in the lugs. As you do this, evenly turn the screws until they are as tight as you can get them with just your fingers. Now, use a drum key to twist each tuning screw half a turn, moving in a clockwise motion around the drum. Be careful not to over-tension any of the tuning screws, since that will affect the overall tension of the drum. At this point, you can begin to tune the drum, either by adjusting the screws in a clockwise direction or by using a cross-tensioning method; both are shown below. You'll notice that the *pitch* (highness or lowness) of the drum rises as you tighten the screws. Continue to turn the screws until you arrive at a tensioning that sounds and feels good to you. Remember that the looser the drumhead, the more difficult it will be to play, since there will be less rebound from the stick. Experiment to find a tuning that you like.

Cross-Tensioning

One way to tune is a method called *cross-tensioning*. This system maintains even tensioning around the drum throughout the tuning process. Tap the head about two inches from each rod to be sure the pitch is consistent around the drum. If it is not, adjust individual tension rods as needed.

The numbers show the order in which the tension rods are tuned.

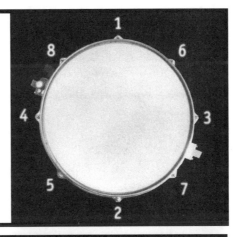

Clockwise Tensioning

You can also tune the drum in a clockwise fashion. Start at 1 and tighten each rod one half turn each time. Do this until the drumhead feels firm. Again, tap the head about two inches from each rod to be sure the pitch is consistent around the drum.

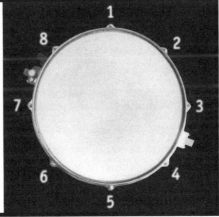

Getting the Whole Set in Tune

It's a good idea to tune your set by beginning with either the lowest drum (bass drum) and tune the remaining drums from lowest pitch to highest, or to begin with the highest drum (usually the snare) and tune the remaining drums from highest pitch to lowest. Experiment to get an overall sound that you like.

● Holding the Drumsticks

Here are two ways of holding the sticks. Try both to see which works best for you.

Matched grip

Matched grip is a very natural and effective technique in which both hands hold the sticks in the same exact way.

Grip the stick between the thumb and first joint of the index finger. Hold it about a third of the way—that is, about five inches—up from the butt, which is the thickest end of the stick. Use the other three fingers to help control the stick.

Matched Grip

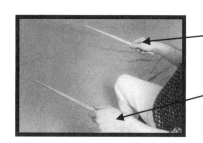

Make sure to avoid too much tension in the hands; keep this gap between thumb and index finger open.

To play, turn the hand so that the back of the hand is facing upward.

Don't grip the sticks too tightly; play with just enough tension to be able to hold and control the stick. Be sure to maintain the gap shown in the photo above.

To play, turn your hand so that the back of the hand faces upward. Your wrist should be able to move up and down freely and naturally. Think of the stick as an extension of your hand.

Traditional grip

In the traditional grip, the right hand holds the stick as in the matched grip, while the left hand holds the stick in a sideways fashion as described below. (If you are left-handed, you may choose to reverse these instructions.) Many jazz drummers use this method of playing, which originated in the days when military drummers would play snare drums that were slung around the neck and held to the side.

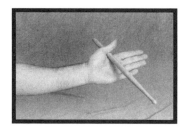

Place the stick in the socket between the thumb and index finger, with one-third of the stick (from the butt end) extending behind the hand.

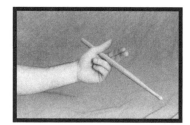

The index and middle fingers should rest lightly on top of the stick to act as a guide. The stick should rest across the ring finger as a support. The pinkie should rest against the middle finger.

View of the traditional grip from the top. The right hand holds the stick as in the matched grip, while the left hand uses the new grip.

● Counting Exercises

The drummer's main function in a musical group is to keep time with precision and consistency. One way you can begin to do this is to practice counting. Have you ever heard a band start a song by having the drummer count 1–2–3–4? This *count off* lets everyone in the band know two important things:

1. What the tempo of the song is.

2. When to start playing.

Let's begin by practicing some important counting exercises that will help you play. First, count aloud, 1–2–3–4, 1–2–3–4, over and over, keeping a steady tempo.

Once you're able to do this verbal count, move on to playing on the snare drum. (You can also use a practice pad, which is a rubber mat that allows you to practice when no drum is handy.) Count 1–2–3–4 as you play with just the right hand, hitting the drum as you say each number. (If you're left handed, you can reverse these instructions.) Make sure that your playing and counting are perfectly matched up and that your tempo is steady.

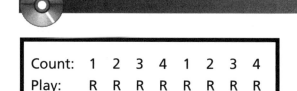

Track 2

Exercise 1

Count:	1	2	3	4	1	2	3	4
Play:	R	R	R	R	R	R	R	R

R = Right hand

Now change the *sticking* (hand pattern) to right–left–right–left, one hand following the other. As before, count out loud: 1–2–3–4, 1–2–3–4.

Track 3

Exercise 2

Count:	1	2	3	4	1	2	3	4
Play:	R	L	R	L	R	L	R	L

L = Left hand

Try tapping your foot to the count. To begin, just tap your foot without playing to get a feel for it.

Track 4

Exercise 3

Count:	1	2	3	4	1	2	3	4
Tap:	F	F	F	F	F	F	F	F

F = Foot tap

Once you can do Exercise 3 comfortably, play along with your foot tapping. Again, use R–L–R–L sticking. Continue counting aloud to make sure that you keep a steady tempo.

Exercise 4

Track 5

Count:	1	2	3	4	1	2	3	4
Play:	R	L	R	L	R	L	R	L
Tap:	F	F	F	F	F	F	F	F

Continue tapping your foot and counting aloud, but play only on the "1" count, using your right hand.

Exercise 5

Track 6

Count:	1	2	3	4	1	2	3	4
Play:	R				R			
Tap:	F	F	F	F	F	F	F	F

Continue tapping your foot and counting aloud, but play only on the "2" count.

Exercise 6

Track 7

Count:	1	2	3	4	1	2	3	4
Play:		R				R		
Tap:	F	F	F	F	F	F	F	F

Continue this pattern, playing only on the "3" count.

Exercise 7

Track 8

Count:	1	2	3	4	1	2	3	4
Play:			R				R	
Tap:	F	F	F	F	F	F	F	F

Now try it on the "4" count.

Exercise 8

Track 9

Count:	1	2	3	4	1	2	3	4
Play:				R				R
Tap:	F	F	F	F	F	F	F	F

Reading Music

Beats and Note Values

The counts you've been using are like a steady pulse, which in music is called the *beat.* The number of beats is shown with *note values.* Here are some of the note values you'll run into most often.

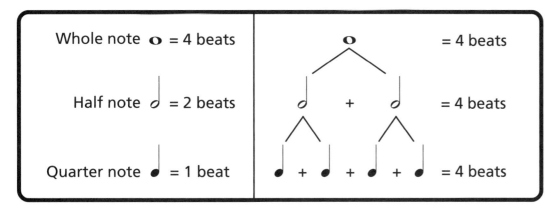

In this book, the quarter note will always receive one beat. It is by combining long and short note values that *rhythm* is created, so learn them well.

The Staff

All the music in this book is written on a *staff* of five lines and four spaces. The symbol at the beginning of the staff, which looks like two vertical lines, is called a *drum clef.* The drum clef tells you that the music on the staff is for drums. Each line and space represents a different instrument in the drum set.

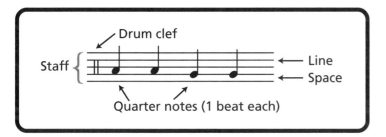

Measures

Beats are grouped into *measures* of equal length—that is, each measure contains the same number of beats. Measures are marked off with vertical *bar lines.* In this book, most exercises will end with a *double bar line.*

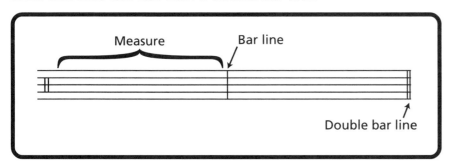

Time Signatures

At the beginning of every exercise in this book, you'll find a time signature. A *time signature* tells you how many beats are contained in each measure. The top number tells you how many beats are in each measure; the bottom number tells you which note value gets one beat. The time signature for all the Exercises in this book is $\frac{4}{4}$:

4 = Four beats per measure
4 = Quarter note gets one beat

Here's an example of music in $\frac{4}{4}$. Notice that each measure adds up to four beats.

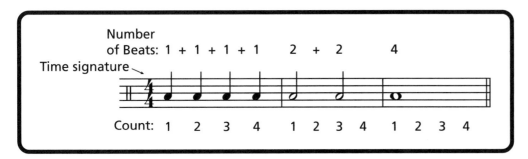

The Quarter Rest

Each note value has a corresponding rest. A *rest* is a musical silence; when you come across a rest, simply stop playing for the value of the rest. Though you won't play during rests, they remain part of the count. Be sure to always give them their full value.

The first rest you'll need to know is the *quarter rest.* Like the quarter note, the quarter rest is equal to one beat:

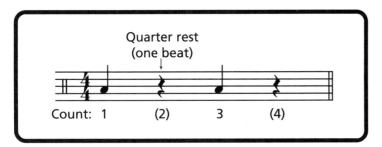

● Repeat Signs

This is a repeat sign: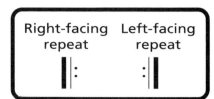

Repeat signs are a way of saving space in music. When you come to a repeat sign, go back to the beginning of the exercise and play again from there. Sometimes, only part of an exercise is repeated. When that happens, repeat signs surround the measures that are to be repeated. The first will have two dots on the right side, and the other will have dots on the left.

Right-facing repeat	Left-facing repeat

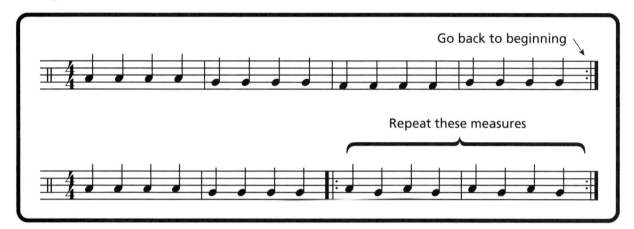

● Snare Drum Exercises

Here's an exercise that uses a little bit of everything you've learned so far. First, you'll be playing on the snare drum. Music for the snare drum will be notated on the third space up from the bottom of the staff:

As you play through this exercise, it's a good idea to count aloud and tap your foot so that you'll always know where you are in a measure and will be able to keep a steady tempo. Try to read slightly ahead as you play so that you can anticipate what comes next. Remember to give quarter rests their full value as you count.

Exercise 9

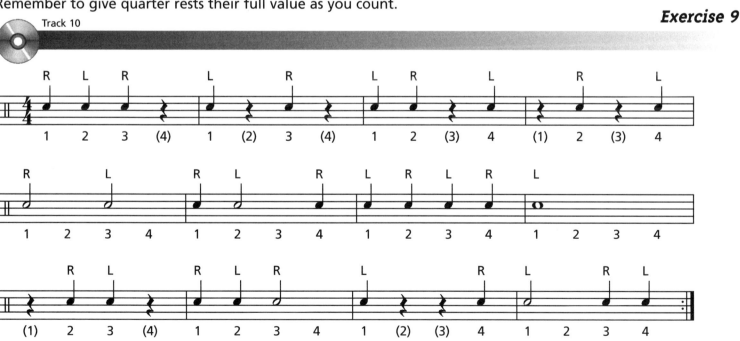

● Half Rests and Whole Rests

The next exercise uses two new rests, the *half rest* and the *whole rest*. Like the half note, the half rest has a value of two beats. The whole rest has a value of four beats. Notice that while they have a similar appearance, the half rest rests on the third line of the staff, while the whole rest hangs down from the fourth line. The whole rest fills out measures in which you don't play at all. As with quarter rests, be sure to give half rests and whole rests their full value as you count.

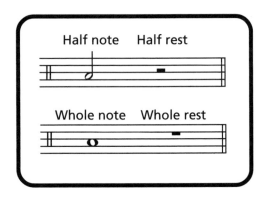

Here's an exercise that uses combinations of all of the note and rest values you've learned. Count aloud as you play, and be sure to continue counting during rests.

Exercise 10

Track 11

Eighth Notes

By dividing a beat in half, you can get an even smaller note value than the quarter note. This note value is the *eighth note*.

Single eighth notes look like quarter notes with the addition of a *flag*. Groups of eighth notes are attached by a heavy line called a *beam*.

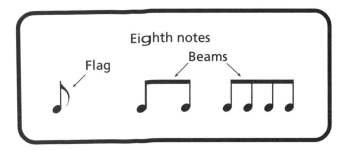

Since you count quarter notes 1–2–3–4, and eighth notes are half as long as quarter notes, count eighth notes like this ("&" = "and"): 1 & 2 & 3 & 4 &. Think of tapping your foot: The number counts are your foot going down, and the "&" counts are your foot going up.

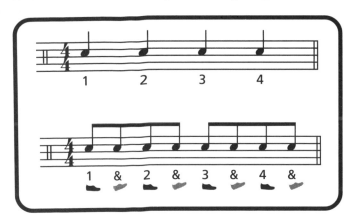

Here's an exercise that will help you feel the transition between quarter notes and eighth notes. Play a measure of quarter notes with just the right hand, followed by a measure of eighth notes with an R–L–R–L sticking pattern. Notice that when you play eighth notes, your right hand plays on all the number counts, while your left hand plays on the "&" counts. Repeat this exercise several times to get comfortable with this transition from quarter notes to eighth notes and back.

Exercise 11

Track 12

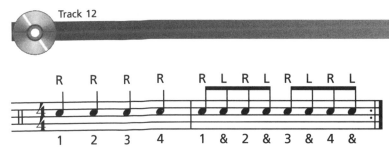

Basic Techniques

● Basic Stroke Technique

Here are a few suggestions for getting your hands to sound even as you play. First, make sure that both hands are at the same height as they prepare to make a stroke, and that they return to the same height. If one hand is higher than the other, your strokes won't sound even.

Correct   Incorrect

As you play the snare drum or any drum in your set, strike in the center of the head to achieve a full drum sound. Make sure that your strokes travel in a straight line, directly down into the head. As you practice, watch your sticks so that you don't hit them together.

Correct   Incorrect

Don't squeeze or pinch the sticks as you hit the drum, and try to avoid any unnecessary tension in your grip. This will result in a better sound and make it easier to build up speed and endurance. Make the sticks do most of the work; allow them to rebound off the drum rather than "choking" them on the drumhead.

PHOTO • JOE SIA/COURTESY OF STAR FILE PHOTO, INC.

Neil Peart is the drummer and lyricist for the Canadian rock trio Rush, an immensely popular group since the mid-1970s. His flawless technique and fluency in playing in unusual time signatures are two of the elements that give the group its characteristic sound.

● Rudiment: The Single-Stroke Roll

Rudiments, the basic playing vocabulary of the drums, have been around for years. The first rudiment we'll look at is the *single-stroke roll*. The single-stroke roll uses one stroke per hand: R–L–R–L. (Left-handed players can reverse these instructions—that is, start with the left hand and alternate the hands.) Listen as you play to make sure that your playing is even and that the hands sound the same.

Here's an Exercise of the single-stroke roll using quarter notes:

Exercise 12

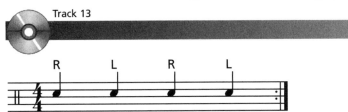

Here's an exercise of the single-stroke roll using eighth notes:

Exercise 13

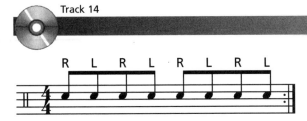

Exercise 14 begins with quarter notes and changes to eighth notes. Be sure to maintain the single-stroke sticking as you make the transition.

Exercise 14

This exercise will help develop your ability to play the single-stroke roll. Remember that each half note has a value of two beats.

Exercise 15

● Rudiment: The Double-Stroke Roll

The next rudiment is the *double-stroke roll.* The double-stroke roll is played as two even strokes per hand. Play through this exercise a few times to get used to the feeling of the double-stroke roll.

Exercise 16

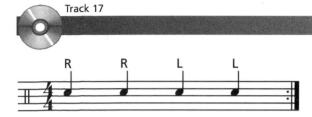

Here's an exercise of the double-stroke roll using eighth notes. Make sure that you keep a steady tempo and listen for evenness between the hands.

Exercise 17

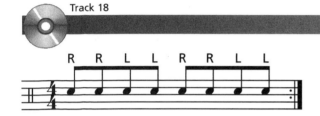

This exercise includes both quarter-note and eighth-note double strokes. As you practice, make sure that the second stroke in each hand is even with the first. With practice, you'll be able to develop this into a nice-sounding roll.

Exercise 18

The next exercise combines the single-stroke and the double-stroke rolls. Make sure that both rolls sound the same and that the hands are even as you play.

Exercise 19

● Rudiment: The Paradiddle

The *paradiddle* is a combination of single and double strokes. The sticking pattern for the paradiddle is R–L–R–R–L–R–L–L.

You can also relate the way the paradiddle is played to the sound of its name. Think of the syllables "pa" and "ra" as single strokes, and "diddle" as a double stroke :

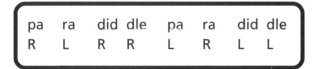

pa	ra	did	dle	pa	ra	did	dle
R	L	R	R	L	R	L	L

Here's an exercise that includes paradiddles in both quarter notes and eighth notes.

Exercise 20

Track 21

Accents

An *accent* is a musical stress. Notes with an accent mark (>) should be played louder (with slightly more force) than the surrounding notes. In the next exercise, use the same paradiddle sticking you already know, and be sure to accent only those notes that include an accent mark.

Exercise 21

Track 22

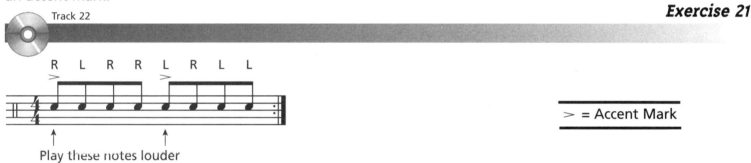

Play these notes louder

> = Accent Mark

Lars Ulrich, drummer for the band Metallica since the 1980s, is known for fast and furious double-bass drumming and high-energy performances.

● The Eighth Rest

The next exercise uses a new rest, the *eighth rest*. The eighth rest has exactly the same value as an eighth note—that is, half a beat. Here's what the eighth rest looks like:

Eighth rest

The next exercise will help you become more familiar with eighth notes and eighth rests. Since eighth rests have the same value as eighth notes, you'll count them as you do eighth notes—1 & 2 & 3 & 4 &, etc. Be sure to maintain a steady count throughout, and, as with the other rests you know, be sure to give the eighth rest its full value. The count is written for you under the first four measures. You might find it helpful to write it out under the remaining measures.

Track 23

Exercise 22

Count: 1 & (2) 3 & (4)   1 & (2) & (3) & (4) &   (1) & 2   3   4   (1)   2 & 3 & (4) &

etc.

● Rudiment: The Three-Stroke Roll

The *three-stroke roll* is a combination of one single stroke and one double stroke. Here are two variations on the three-stroke roll:

Track 24

Exercise 23

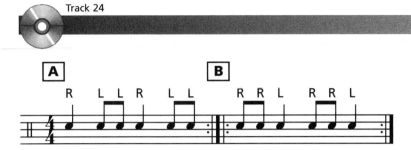

Try this exercise that uses the three-stroke roll:

Track 25

Exercise 24

Exercises 25 and 26 are similar to Exercise 23, but use an alternating single-stroke sticking. Playing similar rhythms with different stickings increases your technical flexibility and gives you more options when performing. For some passages, in fact, any number of stickings might be possible.

Track 26

Exercise 25

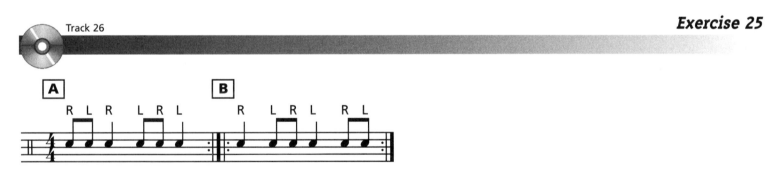

Track 27

Exercise 26

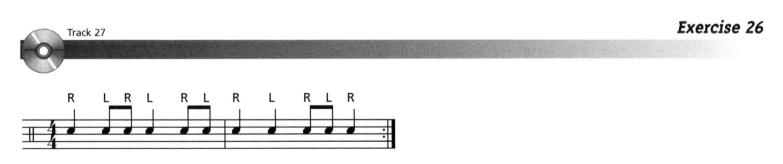

Review Exercise

This exercise includes a little of everything you've learned to this point. Take your time and choose a tempo that's slow enough for you to be able to play accurately. When you're able to play the exercise consistently, without any mistakes, try increasing the tempo a little. Be sure to observe all the sticking indications and don't forget to count—especially during rests!

Track 28

Tommy Lee gained worldwide recognition in the 1980s as the drummer for the band Mötley Crüe. He has a solid rock style and is a master showman on the drums.

PHOTO • JEFFREY MAYER/COURTESY OF STAR FILE PHOTO, INC.

The Next Steps

● The Metronome

A *metronome* is an adjustable device used to keep steady time and to find musical tempos with great precision. Since a metronome doesn't slow down or speed up, it's a helpful tool in checking the accuracy and evenness of your rhythm. If you've never played with a metronome, it may feel a little strange at first—unlike humans, after all, a metronome's sense of timing is perfect. The key to using the metronome is to "lock in" with the metronome's tempo. By concentrating on keeping the beat set by the metronome, you'll become more aware of whether you're *rushing* (speeding up) or *dragging* (slowing down). Here are two metronome exercises to try.

For Exercise 28, set the metronome to 92. Numbers on the metronome indicate beats per minute. The marking ♩ = 92 means that each quarter note gets one tick with the metronome set at 92 beats per minute.

Play quarter notes, one note per tick of the metronome, using a single-stroke roll sticking. Each note should fall directly on the metronome's beat.

Track 29

Exercise 28

♩ = 92

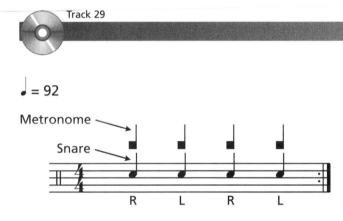

Now, keeping the metronome at the same setting, play eighth notes (two notes per metronome tick) using a single-stroke roll sticking. Again, your right-hand notes should fall right on the metronome's beat.

Track 30

Exercise 29

♩ = 92

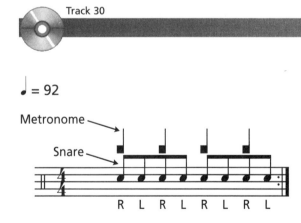

When you're comfortable with both exercises at this tempo, move the metronome setting up to 100 and try them again. All the exercises you'll find later in this book include a suggested tempo marking in the top left-hand comer. With time and patience, playing with a metronome will become easier—and you'll actually have fun!

Accent Patterns

In the following exercises, you'll play a steady stream of eighth notes using a single-stroke-roll sticking and add accents within the roll. Playing accents will help build control between your hands and give the rhythm some variety.

Try this exercise:

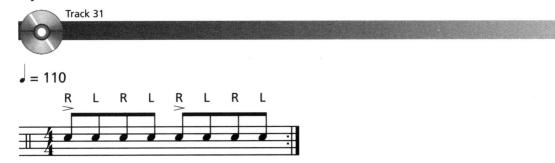

Track 31

Exercise 30

Notice that the right hand plays this accent line:

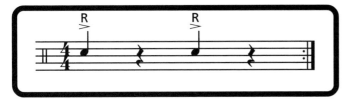

Now try this pattern, which includes accents in both hands. Take it slow and make sure that you're placing the accents accurately.

Track 32

Exercise 31

Here are a few more accent patterns to work on. Be sure to make a clear distinction between accented and unaccented strokes; they should sound different from each other.

Track 33

Exercise 32

Let's continue with more accent patterns. Take your time as you play. Begin the exercises slowly, then play them faster as you gain control over the patterns. Be sure that the correct hand is playing the accents as indicated above the exercises. Have fun!

♩ = 120

Mitch Mitchell played the drums with the Jimi Hendrix Experience beginning in 1966 and continued with them until Hendrix's death in 1970. Mitchell's fluid funk/jazz/rock style was a perfect match for Hendrix's superb guitar playing.

PHOTO • JIM CUMMINS/COURTESY OF STAR FILE PHOTO, INC.

Sixteenth Notes

Now it's time to move on to *sixteenth notes*. Sixteenth notes are half as long as eighth notes. Single sixteenth notes have two flags; groups of sixteenth notes have two beams.

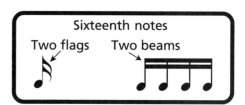

Sixteenth notes
Two flags   Two beams

Take a look at the relationship between quarter notes, eighth notes and sixteenth notes. Notice how sixteenths are counted: 1 e & a, 2 e & a, etc.

Quarter notes: One per beat

Eighth notes: Two per beat

Sixteenth notes: Four per beat

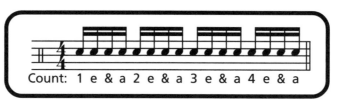

Here's an exercise that will help you play sixteenth notes. First, play quarter notes with your right hand:

Track 35

Exercise 34

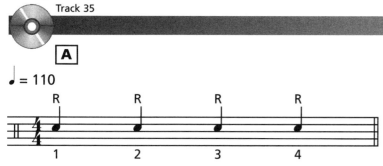

Now, keeping the same tempo, play eighth notes with your right hand:

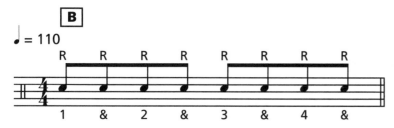

Finally, still at the same tempo, use your left hand to place a note between all your right-hand eighth notes. You'll be playing sixteenth notes!

Sixteenth-Note Exercises

Below are some exercises to help you become more familiar with sixteenth notes. The first is the single-stroke roll in eighth notes, and then in sixteenths. Take your time, and listen to make sure that you're playing the rhythms accurately.

Track 36

Exercise 35

Now, try the double-stroke roll in eighth notes, and then in sixteenths. Make sure those double strokes are even!

Track 37

Exercise 36

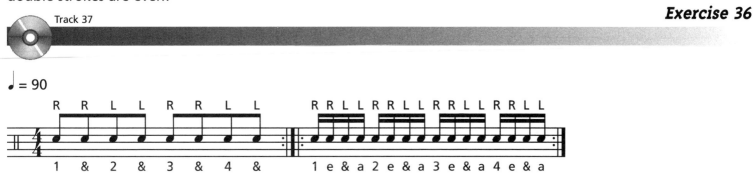

Rudiment: The Five-Stroke Roll

The *five-stroke roll* will be your next rudiment. It can be played with either single or double strokes. First, try the five-stroke roll in eighth notes.

Track 38

Exercise 37

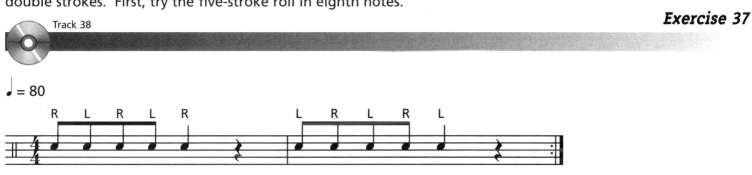

Now, try the five-stroke roll in sixteenth notes. The first time through, use a single-stroke sticking; the second time through, use a double-stroke sticking.

Track 39

Exercise 38

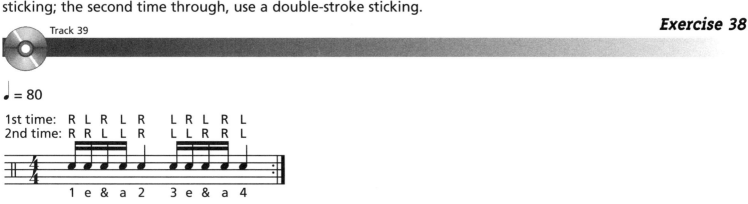

Rudiment: The Six-Stroke Roll

The *six-stroke roll* is a rudiment that uses a combination of note values in a pattern of six strokes. Let's begin with the six-stroke roll in eighth notes and quarter notes. The first time through, use a single-stroke sticking; the second time through, use a double-stroke sticking.

Track 40

Exercise 39

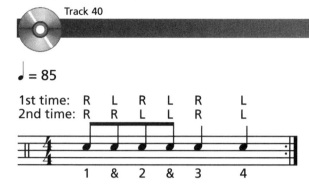

Now, try the six-stroke roll using sixteenth notes and eighth notes.

Track 41

Exercise 40

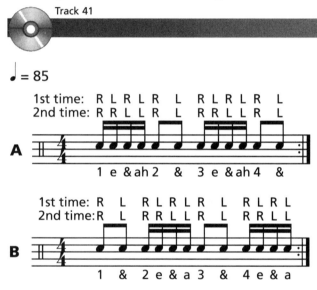

Here's an exercise that combines the six-stroke roll and the five-stroke roll. Be sure to play evenly and to maintain a steady tempo throughout.

Track 42

Exercise 41

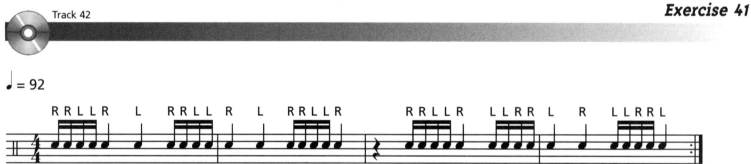

● More Sixteenth-Note Exercises

Here's an exercise that will help you play single strokes, double strokes and paradiddles in sixteenth- note rhythms. Play each measure four times without stopping. Be sure to count as you play.

 Track 43

♩ = 100

R L R L R L R L R L R L R L R L

R R L L R R L L R R L L R R L L

R L R R L R L L R L R R L R L L

1 e & a 2 e & a 3 e & a 4 e & a   etc.

Sixteenth- and Eighth-Note Mix

These exercises will help you become more familiar with eighth notes and sixteenth notes in combination. Play these exercises slowly at first and make sure that the rhythms are absolutely accurate.

 Track 44

♩ = 100

R L R L R L R L R L R L R L   R L R L R L R L R L R L R L   R L R L R L R L R L R L R L   R L R L R L R L R L R L R L L

Track 45

♩ = 100

R L R L R L R L R L R L   R L R L R L R L R L R L R L   R L R L R L R L R L R L   R L R L R L R L R L R L R L

Ginger Baker *was the drummer for the 1960s British rock group Cream, which also included bassist Jack Bruce and guitarist Eric Clapton. Cream defined the power-trio approach to rock music and pushed the envelope in rock improvisation. Baker's fiery extended solos were a highlight of their concerts.*

Combination Exercises

Let's try some exercises that combine concepts and skills you've already worked on. The following exercises are in a march or "street beat" style. These kinds of beats are often used by marching bands and drum corps. Observe the stickings and be sure your rhythms are accurate. Enjoy!

Exercise 45

Track 46

♩ = 110

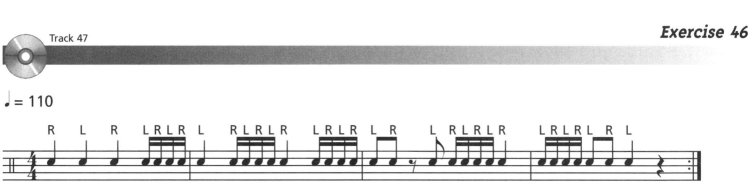

Exercise 46

Track 47

♩ = 110

Exercise 47

Track 48

♩ = 140

Keith Moon *was the drummer for the British rock supergroup The Who in the 1960s and 1970s. The Who recorded many hit records, and their landmark rock opera/concept album* Tommy *helped cement their reputation as one of the great acts of popular music.*

Getting Started on the Drumset

Now it's time to move on to playing on the full drumset. The following suggestions will help you get started.

● Sitting at the Drumset

When setting up your drumset, it's a good idea to place the throne close enough so that both feet can easily reach both the hi-hat pedal (which, for right-handed players, is played by the left foot) and the bass drum pedal (played by the right foot). The snare drum should be directly in front of you and easily within reach. As you sit on the throne behind your set, you'll want to feel balanced as you reach for the different drums and pedals. It's a good idea to set up your drums close enough to you so that you won't have to reach far in order to play them. In the end, coming up with the perfect setup is a matter of trial and error. Each player is built differently, and what works for one may not work for another. Take the time to find a setup that feels comfortable to you.

● Basic Drumset Notation

The following table will help you with the drumset notation used in this book. Notice that, with the exception of the stepped hi-hat, the instruments appear on the staff according to their relative highness and lowness—that is, lower-pitched instruments like the bass drum appear on the lower lines and spaces, while as you move higher on the staff, the pitch of the instruments goes up. Refer to the photo on page 4 if you need to review the instruments in the drumset. Notice that the stems go up for instruments played with the hands, while the stems go down for instruments played with the feet.

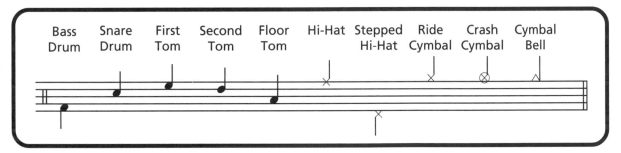

Alex Van Halen, along with his brother, guitarist Eddie, formed Van Halen, one of the most popular rock groups of all time, in the 1970s. Alex is known for his signature sound and his large, multi-tom drumset.

Playing the Bass Drum

The bass drum is played by placing your foot on the pedal and pressing down. There are two ways to play the bass drum: heel up or heel down. With your heel up, you'll have more power coming from your leg. With your heel down, you'll be flat-footed, and you'll have a different sense of balance and sensitivity. Work on both of these techniques, and use the one that works best for you.

Heel up

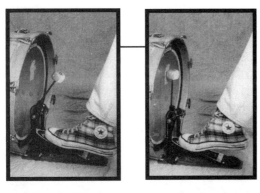

Heel down

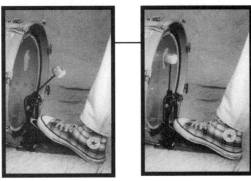

Try the following exercises to get started on the bass drum. First, play quarter notes on the bass drum at a medium tempo.

 Track 49

Exercise 48

♩ = 92

Bass drum

Now, play quarter notes only on beats one and three. Make sure to let the beater on the pedal rebound off of the head of the drum as you play.

 Track 50

Exercise 49

♩ = 92

Playing the Hi-Hat

Let's move on to the hi-hat. To play the hi-hat, depress the pedal to bring the top cymbal down to the bottom cymbal. With practice, you'll get a feeling for how much pressure you need to apply to keep the two cymbals tightly together. Now, with the two cymbals together, cross your right hand over your left, and play quarter notes on the top cymbal, as shown in Exercise 50. You can play the hi-hat with the heel either up or down.

Heel up

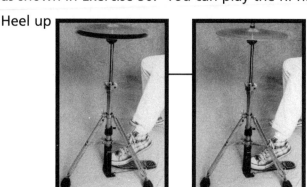

Heel down

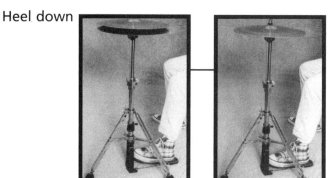

 Track 51

Exercise 50

$\quad$ = 92

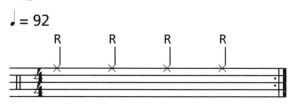

Hi-hat

As you play quarter notes on the hi-hat, use your left hand to add the snare drum on beats two and four. Notice that you're playing the hi-hat and the snare together on these beats. The trick is to hit the two instruments at exactly the same time.

Track 52

Exercise 51

$\quad$ = 92

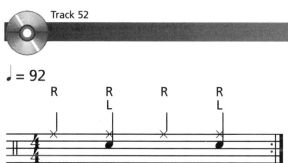

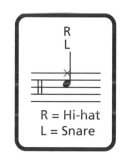
R = Hi-hat
L = Snare

Now, play the hi-hat and the snare drum at the same time in quarter-note rhythms. This will help you get a better feel for crossing your hands to play. Be sure not to hit your sticks together.

Track 53

Exercise 52

$\quad$ = 92

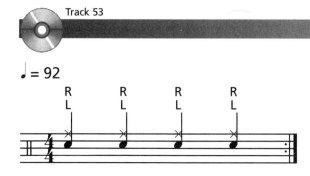

● Adding the Bass Drum to the Hi-Hat

Now it's time to add the bass drum to the quarter-note hi-hat pattern you learned in Exercise 50 on page 33. Make sure to hit the two instruments at exactly the same time.

Exercise 50 on page 33.

Exercise 53

Track 54

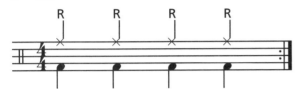

Use your left hand to add the snare drum on beats two and four. Now you're rockin'!

Exercise 54

Track 55

In this exercise, you'll play hi-hat and bass drum on beats one and three, and hi-hat and snare on beats two and four. A snare drum part such as this one, which occurs only on the weak beats of the measure (that is, beats two and four), is often called a *backbeat.*

Exercise 55

Track 56

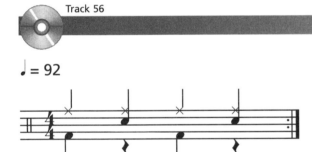

Try playing the bass and snare parts with no hi-hat.

Exercise 56

Track 57

● Eighth Notes on the Hi-Hat

Let's switch from quarter notes to eighth notes on the closed hi-hats. Count the eighth notes as you play, and make sure that the rhythms are even.

Exercise 57

 Track 58

Now, add the snare drum on beats two and four.

Exercise 58

 Track 59

Continue with the pattern from Exercise 58, but add the bass drum on beats one and three.

Exercise 59

Track 60

Now, play the bass drum on all four beats.

Exercise 60

Track 61

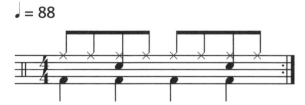

● Bass Drum Variations

The exercises on this page will help you learn to play the bass drum on any beat of the measure as you play the hi-hat and snare. Notice that the bass drum always plays in unison with either the hi-hat or the snare and hi-hat. Take your time, and practice these until they become very comfortable.

Track 62

♩ = 92

Track 63

♩ = 92

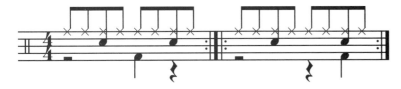

Quarter Notes on the Snare Drum

This drumset beat was popular among 1960s Motown groups such as the Supremes, Smokey Robinson and The Miracles, and others. The snare drum plays a driving quarter note rhythm, the hi-hat plays steady eighth notes and the bass drum comes in on beats one and three.

Track 64

♩ = 110

Here's a variation in which the bass drum plays on all four beats.

Track 65

♩ = 110

● Eighth-Note Rhythms for the Bass Drum

Now you'll begin to play eighth notes on the bass drum. Make sure you're comfortable playing quarter-note rhythms on the bass drum before moving on to this section. Start with the hi-hat and snare parts from the exercises on page 36, and add the bass drum on the first two eighth notes of the measure.

 Track 66

Exercise 65

♩ = 100

Now, add the bass drum on beat three.

 Track 67

Exercise 66

♩ = 100

Once you feel comfortable with Exercise 66, add another eighth note on the "&" of beat three. Notice how the eighth-note bass drum part locks in with the hi-hat rhythm.

 Track 68

Exercise 67

♩ = 100

This exercise includes a single bass-drum kick on beat one and two eighth notes on beat three.

 Track 69

Exercise 68

♩ = 100

This next pattern is a slight variation on the patterns you've already learned. Notice the bass-drum kick on the "&" of beat two. Keep your rhythm steady and make sure that this off-beat kick note is together with the hi-hat. Again, counting as you play will help you learn faster and give you a more solid handle on new material.

Exercise 69

♩ = 92

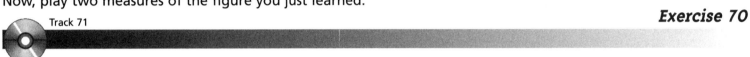

Now, play two measures of the figure you just learned.

Exercise 70

♩ = 92

Here's a slight variation on the idea in Exercise 70.

Exercise 71

♩ = 92

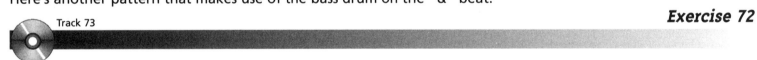

Here's another pattern that makes use of the bass drum on the "&" beat.

Exercise 72

♩ = 92

Beats in a Longer Form

The next exercise uses the drum beats you've already learned in the form of an extended practice exercise. This exercise will help you concentrate on perfecting new material by practicing it over and over. It will also help you make transitions from one beat to the next in a *form* (a set number of measures), much as you would in a real-life playing situation. Begin playing at the indicated tempo; once you're able to play through the exercise with no problems, increase the tempo a little.

Exercise 73

♩ = 110

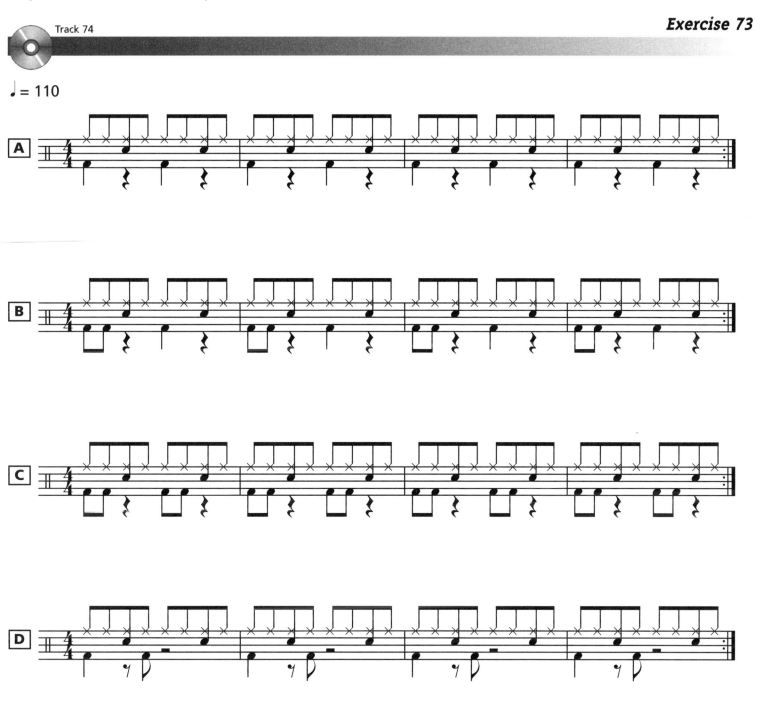

Getting Around the Drumset

Here are a few exercises to help you make your way around the drumset. We'll begin with some exercises for a four-piece set (snare drum, one rack tom, floor tom and bass drum). Begin slowly, concentrating on making your arm movements very smooth and fluid as you go around the set. These exercises use single-stroke sticking, and the bass drum plays on all four beats.

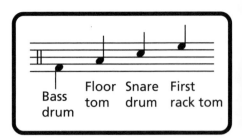

Bass drum · Floor tom · Snare drum · First rack tom

Exercise 74

Track 75

These exercises call for a five-piece set (snare drum, two rack toms, floor tom and bass drum).

Track 76

Second rack tom

Exercise 75

Drum Fills

Now it's time to use a few of the ideas you've learned about getting around the drumset. As songs move from one section to the next, the drummer will often play a passage called a *drum fill* that leads into the next section. Notice that Exercise 76 also shows a way of counting that will help you keep your place as you practice. Notice that the count on the *downbeat* (first beat) of every measure is the number of that measure—that is, the count on the downbeat of the first measure is 1, the count on the downbeat of the second measure is 2, and so on.

Track 77

Exercise 76

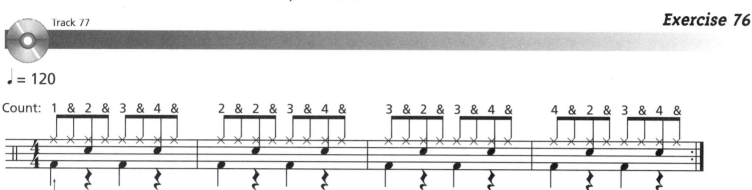

In Exercise 77, you'll play three measures of a drum beat, followed by one measure of a drum fill, for a total of four measures. Be sure to count the measures as you play theses exercises.

Here are some drum fills to try. Count each group of four measures as you did in Exercise 76.

Track 78

Exercise 77

● Crashing the Cymbal

After playing a drum fill, it's often customary to strike the crash cymbal as a kind of musical punctuation. In Exercise 78, you'll use the same form you already know, but this time you'll hit the crash cymbal and the bass drum on the downbeat of the measure following the drum fill. Be sure to maintain a steady tempo throughout; don't rush or drag the fill and cymbal crash.

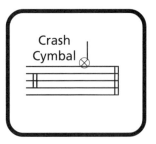

Exercise 78

♩ = 120

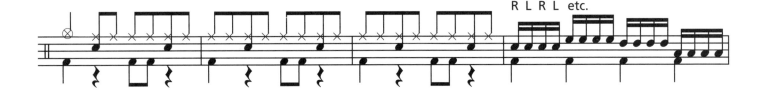

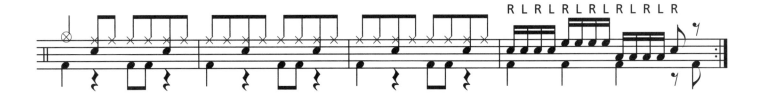

● Playing the Ride Cymbal

Playing the ride cymbal is a great way to add color or change the character of a section of music. Strike the ride about four inches from the edge or, for an additional punch to the sound, on the *bell* (the dome-shaped area in the center). If you're right-handed, the ride cymbal will normally be set up on the right side of the drumset.

Ride cymbal

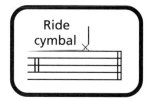

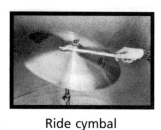

Ride cymbal
(bell)

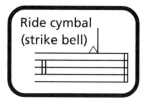

Begin by playing eighth notes on the ride.

Track 80

Exercise 79

Now add the snare and bass drum.

Track 81

Exercise 80

In Exercises 81 and 82, you'll combine playing on the bell with a snare-and-bass-drum groove. If you have difficulty, begin with just the ride part and add the other instruments as you become more comfortable.

Track 82

Exercise 81

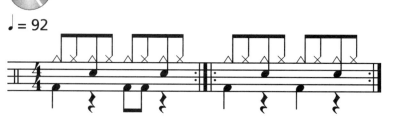

Track 83

Exercise 82

● Stepped Hi-Hat

A great way to play the hi-hat is to use your left foot on the pedal. By using a lot of pressure as you press down the pedal down, you get a "chick" sound, while if you step on the pedal and quickly release your foot, you get a "splash" sound, almost like the cymbals in a marching band. Try playing with both the heel up and the heel down to see which works best for you.

To begin, try stepping some quarter notes on the hi-hat pedal.

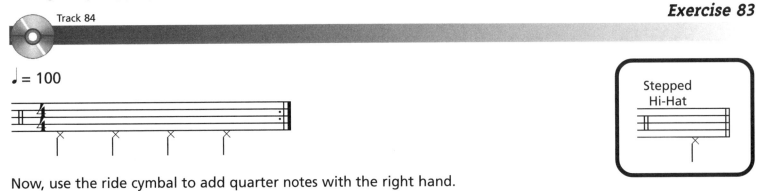

Exercise 83

Track 84

♩ = 100

Now, use the ride cymbal to add quarter notes with the right hand.

Exercise 84

Track 85

♩ = 100

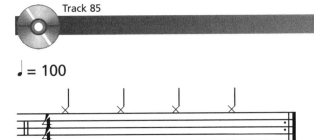

Once you're comfortable with Exercise 84, change the ride-cymbal quarter notes to eighth notes.

Exercise 85

Track 86

♩ = 100

Next, add the bass drum on beats one and three.

Exercise 86

Track 87

♩ = 100

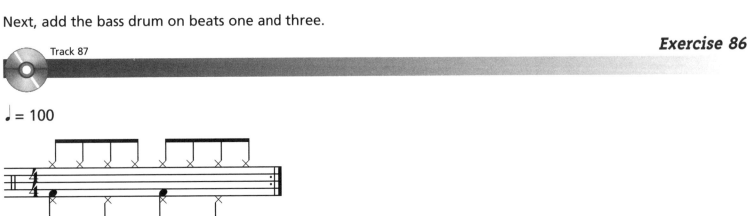

Now, use your left foot to add the bass drum on beats one and three and your left hand to play the snare on beats two and four. Be sure to keep the hi-hat eighth notes locked in with the other parts. Now you're playing with every limb! It may take a while for playing with both hands and both feet at the same time to feel good and natural, but if you stay with it and practice consistently, you'll to master it!

Track 88

Exercise 87

♩ = 100

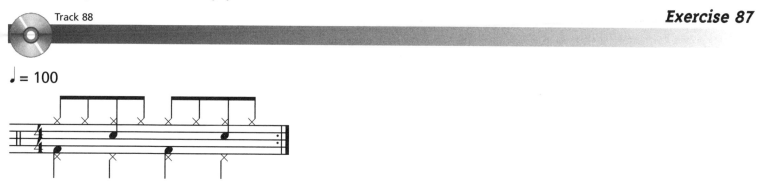

Exercise 88 adds bass-drum eighth notes to the pattern you just played. If you have difficulty with this, simply break down the parts and play with only one limb at a time. Put the rest of the parts together gradually as you become more comfortable.

Track 89

Exercise 88

♩ = 100

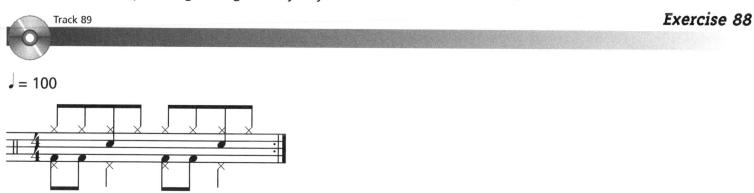

Here are a few exercises in which you'll step on the hi-hat on beats two and four. Notice that the hi-hat part matches up exactly with the snare drum, which also plays on beats two and four.

Track 90

Exercise 89

♩ = 100

● Open and Closed Hi-Hat

In the next few exercises you'll learn how to open and close the hi-hat cymbals for different effects as you play. To get started, try this groove in which the right hand plays the closed hi-hat.

Exercise 90

 Track 91

♩ = 110

Try the same groove again, this time leaving the hi-hat slightly open as you play. To do this, release some of the tension with your left foot.

Exercise 91

 Track 92

♩ = 110

> ∅
>
> Half-open
> hi-hat

Exercise 92 goes back and forth between closed and open hi-hats.

Exercise 92

 Track 93

♩ = 110

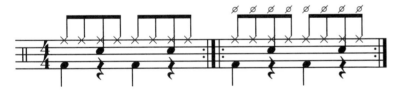

Now you'll play eighth notes as you alternate between the open and closed hi-hat. Open and close the high hat by stepping on and releasing the pedal in a steady rhythm.

Exercise 93

 Track 94

♩ = 100

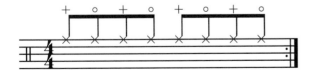

> ○ = Open
> + = Closed

Once you can play Exercise 94 with no problem, add the snare drum on beats two and four, and the bass drum on all four beats. This groove, common in disco music, is a great workout for your left foot.

Track 95

Here's the same groove, this time with the bass drum on beats one and three only.

Track 96

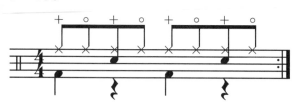

In this groove, which you often hear in funk music, the hi-hat opens on the "and" of one and the "and" of three.

Track 97

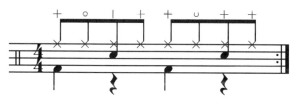

A Few Final Words

I hope you've found the ideas presented in *Drums for the Absolute Beginner* useful, and the exercises fun to play. With practice, you'll be amazed at how much you'll improve—which makes playing the drums even more enjoyable. Remember that everyone learns differently; some people pick things up very quickly, while others need more time. The key to playing well is consistent practice. If you want the music you play to sound natural and flowing, you'll need to practice it over and over. Don't get discouraged if you don't play as well as you would like to right away. Stay with it—with hard work, you'll become the player you want to be.